# Motherhood Moments

# Catherine Burr

Motherhood Moments

Copyright © 2011 by Catherine Burr

ISBN 978-1-892851-63-5

All rights reserved. No part of this book may be reproduced or transmitted in any form or by any means without written permission of the author.

Cover by Night Owl Designs

Published by New Line Press

Printed in the USA

10 9 8 7 6 5 4 3 2 1

Dedicated to my sons,
Timothy Jr., and Daniel,
who make every day of my life a joy!

## Table of Contents

Motherhood Lesson Plan 101 ............................................... 1

College Moments ................................................................ 3

Trekking to School .............................................................. 6

Trees of Life ........................................................................ 8

Flying Apples ..................................................................... 10

School Chaperone .............................................................. 12

Labor Pains ........................................................................ 14

Halloween Magic ............................................................... 16

Birthday Surprise ............................................................... 17

Trick or Treat .................................................................... 18

Christmas Comes Early ..................................................... 20

Thanksgiving Moments ..................................................... 21

Santa Moments .................................................................. 22

Nog Moments .................................................................... 24

Holiday Greetings .............................................................. 25

Cherished Moments .......................................................... 26

Super Bowl ......................................................................... 28

New Year Moments ........................................................... 29

Mother's Day Moments ..................................................... 30

Summer Heat ..................................................................... 32

| | |
|---|---|
| Fishing Moments | 34 |
| Little League Moments | 37 |
| Dog Daze of Summer | 38 |
| Water Wars | 39 |
| CUin5 | 41 |
| Kitty Moments | 43 |
| TTYL | 45 |
| Watering the Carpet | 47 |
| Disneyland Moments | 49 |
| Soaring Kids | 51 |
| Cat People | 53 |
| Kids Tell All | 54 |
| Caller ID | 55 |
| Tooth Fairy Moments | 56 |
| The DMV | 58 |
| The Mommy Wars | 60 |
| Letting Go | 61 |
| Jellyfish Moments | 63 |
| Advice from Son | 64 |
| Tattoo Moments | 66 |
| No TV, No Problem | 68 |
| Motherhood Ironies | 70 |

Highchair Moments ................................................................ 72
Please Enjoy the Music ......................................................... 73
Taking Care of Grandpa ....................................................... 75
Flying Pennies ........................................................................ 78
About the Author .................................................................. 80
Acknowledgements ............................................................... 81
Books by Catherine Burr ...................................................... 82

# Motherhood Lesson Plan 101

One of the many awesome things about kids is that they live in the here and now. They don't live in the past and they don't worry about tomorrow.

I think we, as adults, can learn a few things from children, like how to get along. That's one of the first things they teach in pre-school – how to share. We teach our children not to clobber someone over the head with a plastic hammer (yes that really happened but we won't discuss that here). But the point is why should we as adults settle for anything less than what we teach our children?

A few basic rules taught in kindergarten: Be a good listener. Be a good helper. Be a team player. Walk don't run. Be respectful. A place for everything and everything in its place. Follow directions. Every day is a fresh start. Patience is a virtue.

(Ok, so preschoolers may not be patient!) But we as adults can set a good example for our little ones so some day they will grow up to be adults that actually listen to their spouse and put their dirty socks in the hamper. And…be understanding when basketball playoffs begin and their wives high-tail it out the door to get their nails done.

So, the next time you're unbelievably frustrated with something, think back to those basic lessons from childhood. You may just surprise yourself by how your whole day can be turned around for the better. And then again, maybe not…in which case, perhaps it's time for a recess, preferably one including a leisurely island cruise, or a flight to the moon.

# College Moments

This is an open letter to all you moms out there who've just had a child graduate from high school. Now that you're preparing for the day your son or daughter flies the coop, along with your shopping list for items such as those extra-long sheets, tape this homework assignment on the refrigerator for you – that's right you, and use it as a handy reference guide for getting through your child's first year of college.

1. When you say good-bye to your child in the fall, try to contain your delight until you have returned safely home. Then you may throw a party. Your child is probably already throwing a bash in their newly inaugurated dorm room, so there is no reason you can't do the same.

2. Don't be surprised if in their first call or e-mail home, they ask for money before they say, "I miss you" or "I love you." Do not be dismayed. This is normal college student behavior. Just know that they do miss and love you even though they won't admit to it. With this knowledge in hand, get out your checkbook and start writing. Checks. Lots of checks.

3. When your child calls and asks, "By the way Mom, what is my major?" Just direct them to the college counseling center. It's the place next to the tuition office that now gets all your money. Remember? You saw it on the orientation tour you attended over the summer.

4. When your college student comes home at Thanksgiving for the first time, make sure you have gone to Costco and bought the largest tub of laundry detergent. Believe me – you'll need it.

5. Be ready over the holidays when your child comes home with an armload of gifts for everyone that they purchased at the college bookstore. Proudly wear the college logo sweatshirt; after all you'll be paying for it once you get the bill.

6. When your college student hands over a stack of parking tickets (even if they don't have a car at school, they will find a way to get them). Try and not clench your teeth as you suggest that they get a job.

7. When you attend parent's weekend, praise your child for a tidy dorm room. It hasn't been that clean since the day they moved in, and won't stay that clean until the day they move out!

8. Try to refrain from calling, text messaging, or e-mailing your college student every single day. Better to send them a bouquet of balloons with, "I love you," vividly displayed on them.

9. Ask to see their report card. Better yet, crack their computer code so you can verify that they have in fact registered for classes in the first place.

10. Last, but not least, be prepared when at the end of their first year of college, you don't recognize your child,

because they're now grown up. Well, almost, three (or four) more years to go!

# Trekking to School

My dad likes to tell the story of how he had to walk for miles to school through the snow. In the prairies of Saskatchewan this was actually true, though sometimes he was living the high life and had a dog team to take him to the one-room wooden schoolhouse.

It must seem like a lifetime ago to today, from the days of dog-sledding to school, like mail carriers, through sleet and snow, to today's world where savvy kids drive BMW's with iPods, cell phones, Starbuck's coffee, and a back pack so heavy they practically need a forklift to carry their books to class.

Yes, things have changed. From my dad forging through the snow to school, to the next generation of my sister and I taking a city bus to school, then walking a few blocks. That thought now would be unacceptable to kids going to school by themselves for heaven's sake, and I think parents are more protective and do not want their children to walk to school, like a time in the not so distant past.

My brother used to question me all the time - why couldn't my kids ride their bikes to school, he wanted to know, like he did when he was a kid? I tried in vain to explain to him that that would mean they would have to cross freeways, busy roads, traffic galore, and the least of which they'd have to get up at the crack of dawn.

I preferred to drive to school to drop my kids off, even half asleep (me, not my kids), but the best part of the day for me, came at days end, because us moms would arrive at the school a few minutes early and stand around and chat and chat and chat, or as the kids would say, gossip. At least until the kids came running out from school, and we'd be ready to do it all again tomorrow (us moms, not the kids!)

# Trees of Life

We were out to breakfast this morning when my mother asked me a simple enough question, "Had I noticed the beautiful trees along the highway?"

"Yes, I had noticed," I responded. "They're quite beautiful," I noted emphatically.

Later that day, as I was driving along the same highway, I realized that I hadn't really noticed the transforming splendor of the forest around me. I drive by them everyday, but the changes they go through merely passed me by. So much of their metamorphic wonderment was outside of my cognate perception. The change was too slow, too gradual and left me not really noticing the beauty and wonderment that they truly hold.

Like the trees, people change, too. Sometimes circumstances change a person's life in an instant, sometimes it's over the course of a lifetime. Sometimes, like the changing of seasons, it sort of sneaks up on us and we stand in awe, asking, "What happened?"

"How did my kids grow up so fast?" "How did my life change so much?" During times like these, when someone asks us if we have seen the beautiful trees along the highway, perhaps what they are saying is -- like the seasons, life changes. Whether we want it to or not, and life goes on. Spring will follow the approaching winter, roses will bud and bloom in renewal. The trees, too, will regenerate their leaves before their next nap for yet the next winter, and the cycle entreats us with a majestic beauty, albeit a very subtle one.

Some trees, strong and stubborn, remain green and lush while others sustain their process of change. Half the trees are filled with green leaves while other leaves on the same tree have already turned into a sunburst of yellow and tints of gold and earthly brown.

I couldn't help but wonder how we, all of us, change and endure the seasons of our own lives. Had I not noticed that higher beauty around me? I thought how quickly my children had grown and now as I reflected on their grandmother's insightful question…Yes, I did see the trees on my drive into breakfast, and they were very beautiful. And… Thanks mom. The trees were even more beautiful as I lolly-gagged home…

## Flying Apples

My son called the other day posing an interesting question. He wanted to know if he or his brother had ever misbehaved while eating out in restaurants when they were little. His inquisitive search caused me to scan my memory back through a bunch of motherhood years. When I reached bibs and booster seats, I still had no particular incident standing out in this playful recollection. My mind had drawn a blank.

I thought of the occasional loosening of a salt and peppershaker lid, but what kid hasn't done that while their parent (or waiter) wasn't looking. Yes, he wanted something concrete, something substantial, and something solid. Hmm, like an apple…

I received call from the school, the nurse was saying: There has been an "incident at school…" With those words, she definitely gained my full and undivided attention.

Oh! My son is fine? But he'd hurt his jaw? What happened? I worried. I fretted. The nurse hee-hawed to explain; there had been a food fight, during lunch, in the cafeteria. A flying object struck my son. Oh? I asked again, "Is he okay? Tell me … Quickly!"

Of all the various food groups, a flying apple had found my son's jaw. After-scare relief flashed through me, I tried with open effort not to laugh.

By the way, here's a piece of parental wisdom, it is easier to get in to see an oral surgeon when it's the same doctor that pulled out your child's wisdom teeth. Thankfully, no surgery was needed -- that day, jaw, teeth or otherwise. But, hopefully, a lesson had been learned. If you pack apples in your child's school lunch, make sure the apples are sliced. If you do pack a solid apple, well… You may be sending a food fight victim scrambling off to an oral surgeon.

P.S. No, it wasn't my son's apple. And no, no one knew who started the food fight. But, I'm sure that -- my son -- had nothing to do with it!

## School Chaperone

I don't know what made me think about it today, I guess maybe cause summer is around the corner and I was thinking about how it means freedom for moms from making lunches, chaperoning to and from school, and going on – oh, all those field trips.

But, then I recalled how my field trip chaperoning days ended quite abruptly. No, not because I was fired from a volunteer position, though I've been on enough volunteer committees over the years where discussing how to fire someone else from a volunteer post was vehemently was discussed (but that's another story).

When my son began 5th grade, we had just moved to a new city, a new state, and thus a new school for him. And one of the first things he told me was that my days of volunteering were over! He politely said, "Mom, you've done enough."

Looking back, I wonder what he really meant by that. He continued, "Seriously Mom, you've volunteered for years and you don't need to anymore."

At first I kind of upset; my world was turned upside down. Volunteering and being a part of the school atmosphere was my life. I was a stay-at-home mom. I volunteered on committees, baked tasty cupcakes, and… went along on field trips.

I did however respect my son's honesty, his forthright nature, and I took his suggestion under advisement. After that, he did ask me from time to time if I wanted to volunteer for one school outing or another. And with his enthusiastic nature, I took him up on his invite. In retrospect, maybe all along, he just wanted to be asked?

## Labor Pains

Labor Day is the real day when we ought to honor moms. We should honor anyone who has labored laboriously during delivery labor in a laboring experience – giving labor to their baby. That's what Mother's Day is for? I hear you saying. No, I think Labor Day may be much more appropriate.

I shall not regal you in my own tales of labor. I shall not tell you how with my first child, during a laborious labor, I yelled and screamed at my husband, the nurse, the doctor, my own mother, whom I screamed at in particular for not advising me ahead of time how much pain labor would entail. I will not tell you how I removed the fetal monitor for the umpteenth time and hollered in a voice that was reminiscent from the movie "The Exorcist" that I was not having that thing around my waist and I removed it and tossed it across the room.

Once when I fell and broke my ribs and the paramedic asked me on a scale of one to ten, what level my pain was at, I told him it was just like childbirth, it was a ten. Any pain, heaven forbid, once one has endured labor, can and will always be compared to that dramatic experience.

To all those young ladies out there who haven't yet had a child, don't let my labor or any other mother's laborious experience become a deterrent to you in any way. The benefits far out way the labor, and when you hold your own precious little cargo dearly in your arms, you'll forget all about the labor you just went through… Well, not really…but it's still worth it.

## Halloween Magic

One of the things I find ironic about Halloween is that it's the one night of the year we wait until dark to send our children out of the house. And why is it that Daylight Savings Time always ends just before Halloween? And why do I always worry, will I have enough candy for the trick-or-treaters before I've gobbled it up all myself. And most of all will my dentist offer me a discount for this annual influx of sugar upon my teeth?

I find the stages of Halloween interesting. As parents, we can't wait until our little ones are old enough to be stuffed into a little princess or a pumpkin costume. But they are too young to know the difference, and at this stage, it's the parents who are usually holding the bag out for candy – lots of candy.

When our children are school age, costumes become whatever the mass majority are wearing. Half the school may show up in the same costume albeit different versions.

Then comes the high school years when teens trade the house-to-house trick-or-treating for congregating at someone's house, but still like to get their hands in the cookie jar – I mean candy bowl.

Halloween is the one time when we let our kids stay out late – well, not too late. Parents are at home waiting. Waiting for their kids and the candy too.

# Birthday Surprise

I love birthdays. What other time of year do we get to have our cake and eat it too? And presents yet ... got to love those gifts. But sometimes the best gift is the simplest. Sure, who doesn't like to open packages and have balloons and festive décor, but still sometimes a home made gift, a crayoned card, flowers picked from the garden, or a phone call or message from far-a-away, says, "Happy Birthday" more than the most expensive toy money can buy.

Birthday parties for children these days have become an event in and of themselves. I was watching a TV show the other night, and it was like a contest to see who could out do the other with the most expensive party.

I have to admit the most memorable birthdays to me are those with love and care and not much fan-fare! Enjoy birthdays in the simplest of ways!

# Trick or Treat

Halloween is over for another year and besides the usual morning conversations of politics, the news, perhaps the most important question swirling around is, "How many trick-or-treaters did you have at your house?"

This year I did not run out of candy. But I remember the year we did. And it was not pretty. It was barely six-thirty and the trick-or-treaters had already been arriving and the candy bowl was getting low. My son offered to go to the store to get more candy, which he did. In the meantime, I wasn't sure what to do. Hand out dimes? Nickels? Surely not pennies. Should we turn the lights out and run and hide? Put a note on the door? Thankfully the store wasn't too far away and my son soon arrived back home with plenty of candy to surely last the night with leftovers for us to munch on. Except something happened. The trick-or-treaters kept arriving. An endless parade of ghosts and goblins trekking to our door in search of a piece of chocolate, or two.

A debate ensued in our house. Should we race back to the store to buy yet more candy? My son mumbled something and dashed out the door to his own planned festivities. Meanwhile the trick-or-treaters continued to arrive in droves. Suddenly I felt like I was being stingy, lessening the amount of candy handed out with each doorbell ring.

By seven-thirty, we ran out of candy again. But this time we turned the lights out and ran and hid. Okay, we didn't really hide, but we did turn the lights out. And were determined the following year not to eat all the candy before Halloween.

## Christmas Comes Early

I was in the store today and had to do a second-take when I saw Christmas ornaments on the shelf. It's not even Halloween yet? Where were those decorations? Well, I found them soon enough as I turned the corner of an isle, knocking down a scarecrow in the process.

Two little boys, who witnessed my hit and run, looked horrified. "He's okay," I said, picking up the - almost as tall as I am - scarecrow. The youngsters gave me the evil eye. "Really, he's okay," I said, trying to reassure them, but I felt like I'd committed a crime.

As I quickly made my way down the next isle looking for toothpaste, there were Thanksgiving decorations. Thankfully I didn't knock down any turkeys in the process, but I did wonder why stores put these items out so early in the season, and where oh where had the store hidden the toothpaste?

I do have a Christmas story which I can't wait to write about, but I think I'll save it until it gets a little closer to, you know, Christmas…

## Thanksgiving Moments

The last turkey (leftover) sandwich has been consumed, the relatives have headed home, and the biggest shopping day of 2006 is now history and in the wringing hands of statistical and predictable Christmas sales analysts.

What are the odds of finding a Play Station 3 in the next 28 days at all, let alone, on sale? I did read that Santa arrived at the mall by helicopter after the parade. And, the same mall is now beautifully decorated with twinkling lights, reindeers, wreaths, and elves wearing red and white Santa hats.

I am wondering now about this transitional miracle. I may become a Thanksgiving Day activist to make the holiday last longer. You know, make two turkeys for more leftover sandwiches, and make the relatives stay a week... Well, maybe not. After all, we'll all get together again soon enough for December festivities. We will? Yikes! Bring on the nog!

## Santa Moments

Early Christmas morning...my husband and I were still asleep when we heard a knocking on our bedroom door. No, it wasn't Santa, but our young children announcing Santa hadn't arrived yet. Oops. "Go back to bed," we said, "I'm sure he'll be here soon."

I flew out of bed faster than Santa's sleigh racing through the night sky. But what happened? Had Santa missed our house? We'd been good (for the most part) all year. Hopefully no lumps of coal were in our Christmas stockings. I raced out to the living room and surveyed the situation. Peering up the chimney, I noticed that sure enough, there was no sign of Santa.

I went into the kitchen to start the coffee and when I went back into the living room, my eyes widened in with what seemed like with the blink of a Rudolph's nose the room had transformed. The Christmas tree lights twinkled as colorfully wrapped presents surrounded the base of the tree and the stockings hung on the fireplace mantel overflowed with gifts and candy canes.

I ran down the hallway. "Santa's been here," I said as I knocked on my son's bedroom doors.

"You sure?" They questioned, in voices laced with skepticism.

"Yes, I'm sure," I said with spontaneous glee and the assuredness of motherhood itself.

As I watched them race to the tree, my husband delivered to me a cup of freshly ground coffee, and at that very moment I made an early New Year's resolution to send Santa Claus a new alarm clock…one without a snooze button!

## Nog Moments

I had just received an e-mail from a neighbor commenting how pretty the Christmas lights around my house were, when wouldn't you know it, not more than 5 minutes later, the lights all went out. Why is it even with a declaration on the box that states, "These lights will stay lit even if one goes out," there always seems to be a strand or two that will fail to cooperate?

It's kind of like our Christmas tree stand. I don't think a year has gone by when our tree hasn't fallen over at least once. I mean it just wouldn't be the Holidays without the tree falling over.

It's also like when toy instructions read, "Easy to assemble," or worse yet, "No assembly required." This usually translates to 10 pages of indecipherable directions, which even after careful following, you're left with parts missing or extra ones that you toss in to your junk drawer where they'll still be next year.

What I do at this point is to take a deep breath, pour a glass of eggnog, toss a Yule log into the fireplace, sit down with my stack of Christmas letters, and actually read them. One never knows, maybe a friend, acquaintance or distant relative that I only hear from once a year is offering their ski chalet or ocean front Tahitian get-a-way up for the taking; or maybe not. But it's something that I will add to my wish list, along with lights that don't go out, and a tree that stays in a full and upright position.

# Holiday Greetings

I had just opened my day's mail, which included several "Happy Holidays" and "Merry Christmas" cards. My fingertips glistened... sparkle from a glittering Christmas tree, and gold from one of the three magi, had stuck to my hands.

Even the envelopes, colored in reds and greens with postage of our government's cheer, religious oriented stamps competing with the pretty but generic, snowflake stamp, enhanced each envelope.

Several e-cards arrived on my computer. Beautiful these warm wishes and heartfelt transmissions, but costly to print out if I want to display them with the mailed cards. The e-card and musical interlude that accompanies them are pleasant and colorful on the computer monitor, but there's nothing like a real card in a real envelope arriving the old-fashioned way, in the mail.

As I washed off the glitter of the season from my hands, I thought how wonderful it felt to be on so many thoughtful mailing lists. How grand to keep in touch with extended family and friends, and now ... I'm off to pen (well, maybe e-mail) my own Holiday Greetings. "Merry Christmas" to all and may seasonal happiness over-fill your mailbox...on-line and otherwise.

# Cherished Moments

As I sat in church the other day listening to the minister's sermon, one of the things he said was how we should give presents not just at Christmas time but year-round as well. I thought to myself, true, but try telling that to a 5-year old who waits all year to find a plethora of brightly colored packages under the tree and a fat stocking filled with goodies hanging from the mantle.

One of the joyful times of being a parent is seeing the look of excitement as children run to the tree on Christmas morning. In our house, of course no presents can be opened until mom has a cup coffee in hand. That's a steadfast rule. Get the coffee made quickly, settle down around the tree, and enjoy the twinkling lights on the tree and the majesty of the moment. Soon enough, wrapping paper, bows and boxes will be strewn from one end of the room to the other.

Shopping for little ones is easy. One trip to the toy store, an overflowing shopping cart, and you're done. Well, not quite, there's still that long line to wait in to check out, and hours spent wrapping each gift with care (ok, maybe staying up half the night before Christmas wrapping gifts as quickly as you can, hoping you don't run out of tape).

As children become older, for some reason it seems the items on their Santa list become smaller yet more expensive. Why is that, I wonder? As children grow, suddenly the days of loading up a shopping cart at a toy store becomes a distant memory as you move on to stores with smaller shopping carts and higher prices. But one thing one never forgets are the joyful faces on Christmas morning. Even if youngsters prefer playing with wrapping paper and boxes, and older children are glued to their video games, these are cherished memories that last a lifetime.

## Super Bowl

As I watched the Super Bowl, I couldn't help but think about when my sons wanted to play high school football. When my eldest son started high school and wanted to play football I said, "Absolutely not! It's too dangerous."

Then went my second son started high school and wanted to play football, I said, "Okay."

My older son took umbrage at this. "How come you're letting him play football and you wouldn't let me play?" I really didn't have an answer for him – at least a good answer.

Perhaps with each subsequent child we as parents we become more lenient? Or perhaps when my younger son broke his arm playing basketball I thought, "Well, if one can get hurt playing basketball, then one can get hurt playing any sport."

In any case, we as parents make tough decisions everyday. Sometimes our children understand our reasoning – but mostly I think they don't, especially when we're not sure of the answers ourselves.

Parents only do the best they can at any given moment, and we cross our fingers and hope for that winning touchdown, whether on the football field, or in life.

# New Year Moments

And so another year comes to pass as a new one begins. The only thing that stays the same is change. How uninteresting life would be without change in our lives. As we watch our glorious infants turn into "moving a mile a minute" toddlers, and through the school age years and on into high school and college, life moves at a rapid pace. I used to cringe when people would say to me, "children grow up so fast." I'd cringe because while you're raising children, it doesn't seem so fast. But as mother of grown children, to me, they will always be my kids.

As I reflect on that statement – "…they will always be my kids…" in fact I ask myself -- were they ever? From the moment children are born, they're different from one another and each unique in their own amazing ways. Children in fact are not a possession, but a gift. A gift to their parents, their family, the community, and the universe.

And just as children grow and change, people and circumstances change on a daily basis. We never know what the New Year has in store for us, but we can look to the future and all that life has to offer. Someone asked me recently if I'd made my New Year Resolutions. "No," I said, "I don't make once-a-year resolutions, but ongoing ones, ever day. Well maybe not every day, but at least once a year!

## Mother's Day Moments

The gift mom wants for Mother's Day depends on how old her children are because Mother's Day at different stages means completely different things. For example if mom has a newborn or small infant, what she really would love is the gift of an extra hour of sleep!

If mom has toddlers, well, listen up dad, taking the little darlings out on an outing for the day would give mom a chance to rest, and believe me, come nighttime, you may be well rewarded.

Of course, what mother doesn't love chocolates and flowers as Mother's Day gifts? In fact, giving these gifts on a year-round basis for no reason at all other than to say, "I love you and appreciate you" will go a long way with the mom in your house.

Don't be surprised or frustrated if after asking mom what she wants for Mother's Day it doesn't elicit the response you want, or even a response at all. What she really may be thinking is, "I'd like to be left alone for the day," but that's something we, as moms, don't know how to say without offending all parties involved.

Sometimes the best gifts are the ones that don't cost any money at all. Well, okay, what mom doesn't love that diamond pendant necklace? I mean I've been holding out for that one for years now! Attention. Attention! I'm still waiting for one by the way…

Even a phone call, cut flowers, (e-mail and text messages are too impersonal) can bring a smile to mom's face. Especially on Mother's Day, mom wants to feel loved and appreciated. And a diamond necklace ain't bad either!

# Summer Heat

I don't know about where you live but from where I'm sitting, it's been pretty hot hereabouts, of late. As I was driving through town yesterday, I watched the thermometer looming above the bank change from 110 to 111. I had to keep glancing at the temperature gauge in my car which was hovering near that scary red line; the red line that announces, "Hey lady, get ready to call your AAA club for a tow truck."

As I sweated, while running my errands, I reached over for the cold bottle of water I had brought along, and after taking one gulp, I almost gagged from what had, only a few short minutes earlier, would have been a refreshing cool-down drink, was now hot enough to brew a hot cup of tea if I had only brought along a Nestlé's tea bag.

Keeping one eye on the car's swelter gauge, and the other one searching for the nearest McDonald's where I could get a jumbo-sized drink, I couldn't help but think about the time my kids and I were driving through the Mojave Desert while we were moving to a new home in Arizona. We had pulled over to decide whether we should stop at a nearby water park, or suffer our journey onward.

Reluctantly, we decided to press on, and as we crossed the California border and drove into Arizona, I began having second thoughts about passing up that liquid oasis – that beautiful and refreshing water park.

We pulled off to the side of the road and were so thankful that we'd stopped to get plenty of cold water. And right then, I glanced at my son buckled-up in the passenger seat and reached for a jumbo-sized glass of ice water. I don't know if it was the triple-digit numbers of the thermometer, or the wishing we'd have stopped at that water park, but… I poured the glass of water refreshingly over my son's startled head.

His response of course, was to create our own water park -- he laughingly poured a glass of freezing water over my own head. Except he, at twelve years of age, had much more manners than me – his mom, and readily asked for permission first. Amen!

## Fishing Moments

The scenario was this: it was a beautiful, warm, sunny day, and it seemed like a fine day to get out there and do something fun…so my son and I decided to go fishing. First stop, Wal-Mart. After we purchased our fishing licenses, fishing poles, an assortment of bait, which included live worms, we then went to the local deli and picked up sandwiches for lunch. Next stop…the lake. We decided on the reservoir to the north of us because, well, I thought it would be cooler than the lakes at the lower elevations. Little did we know how much cooler.

When we arrived, we went inside the bait shop and rented a boat. The clerk inquired, "Did we bring jackets, cause it's mighty cold out." My son and I glanced at each other, "Oh yes," I said, "We're prepared." Truth was, I hadn't brought a jacket. When we left the house, it was warm and sunny. But suddenly clouds appeared out of nowhere and soon turned dark and ominous.

Grabbing every extra sweatshirt in my son's car that I could find, including his roommate's jacket (who wasn't along, but hey, you leave your jacket in the car – it's fair game), we gathered our fishing gear and lunch. I wondered aloud as I was holding my purse if I should take it along or not? My son took one look at my over-sized purse, shook his head, and mumbled something about why women needed to carry a purse at all. "What do you have in there anyway?" He asked as he lifted it like it was a set of weights and dropped it into the trunk.

Once in the boat, I sat in front of the engine and readied myself to start that monster.

"Well?" My son said, sitting at the other end of the boat.

"Uh," I said, "I don't know how to start this thing. Actually, I don't know how to drive it either."

"What?" My son's voice echoed through the pine trees. "You said you knew how to run the boat."

I had no choice but to confess. "I lied."

Well, it wasn't really a lie, I really thought I'd be able to figure it out, after all, I'd seen my dad start a boat engine a thousand times, so how hard could it be? I mean, my father taught me how to fish, how to tie and bait a hook, how to catch a fish, even how to clean and cook a fish. But, learning how to drive a boat never came to fruition.

So, I turned the helm over to my son, who suddenly seemed to know exactly how to start it, how to drive it, even though he said he'd never driven a boat before. Hmm…must be something in the male genes.

Just as we were about to pull out, or push off, or whatever it's called when you pull away from the dock, those dark clouds turned white and there, in the middle of June, in the boat on the lake, ready to go fishing, it started to snow.

But we weren't going to let a little hail and snow stop us, so off we went, and what a grand time we had.

Once, I even thought I had a fish on the line! But it turned out my line was tangled in the propeller, and my son, shaking his head (again) carefully removed the line and politely asked me to be more careful next time I made a cast.

I'm not even sure if fish bite when it's snowing out, but I know one thing, fishing in a lake in the middle of summer even if it snows is a good way to break in a new pole and learn how to drive a boat at the same time.

While we were out in the lake, I couldn't help but think about my dad and how many times we'd gone fishing and camping. But I really wish I would have paid a little more attention when he wanted to show me how to drive the boat, but I was probably busy looking in my purse for my lipstick.

## Little League Moments

I see you moms out there counting down the days of summer until school starts and home life returns to normal; when the calendar becomes replaced from summer camp schedules to soccer practices, ballet lessons, tutoring sessions for your kindergartner to score well on the SAT.

I have to admit, I've never been one to fill my kids summers with back-to-back activities. I see the value of building forts out of the living room sofas, after all one day Junior may become an architect. Or letting your son cover the kitchen in flour while attempting to make cookies; he may become a chef one day, and you'll be ever so glad not to have to cook anymore.

Once when I'd let my kids have a sleepover the night before a little league game, yikes, did I ever hear about it from the coach when the team lost. For a half a second, I actually felt a twinge of responsibility. But not for long, I don't even remember the stares I received from the other parents. Nope, the memory is long gone…

I do know that I believe in summers free of schedules and time constraints. I mean for the parents, not the kids. If only we did like in other counties and actually took six-week vacations, we'd all start the fall relaxed and refreshed. Then when a mom decides to let her child have that sleepover the night before a soccer game, perhaps the coach would go a little easier on the players, but most of all, on mom.

# Dog Daze of Summer

The Dog Days of August are here. Starting dates for school are already marked on calendars all across the country. Some schools start as early as this week. What ever happened to school starting after Labor Day? But are moms complaining. Nope.

With each passing day that edges toward school starting, little do kids know that their mothers have their own schedules to keep. Their own lives.

Not that mom's are complaining by any means. We love having our kids around all summer. I personally loved it when my kids wanted to go to the beach, the pool, a baseball game, the movies, the Mall, all in one day.

Did I ever complain? Nope. Because I knew that just around the corner, school would be starting. Is the bus here yet?

# Water Wars

I don't know about where you live but from I sit, it's been pretty darn hot. As I was driving through town yesterday, I watched as the thermometer changed from 110 to 111. I had to keep glancing as I watched the thermostat in my car near the scary red line. The line when I know I have to immediately pull the car over to let it cool down or I'll be calling AAA soon for a tow.

I reached for what was a cold bottle of water a few minutes earlier, and now, if only I had a tea bag, I could've had a bottle of hot tea. I couldn't help but think about the time my kids and I were driving through the desert, and just as we crossed the California border into Arizona, I took my jumbo size glass of cold ice water and poured it over my son's head. He was about 12 at the time, and I believe his response was to pour a glass of water over my head. Except, he having more manners asked for permission first.

My cousin had told me of a story how she was at a summer picnic, and there were lots of moms sitting around gabbing, as we do best, and it was one of those hot days, and the kids were running around not seeming to mind the hot weather. Her daughter (or was it her son? Not sure on that one), but her child came over to her as she sat amongst the other moms at a picnic table and asked if she (or he) could toss a bucket of cold water on her. "Of course," she said. And she was promptly doused with cold water, and horrified stares from the other mothers who couldn't understand why she would let her child pour water over her.

On days when it's 111 out, I can completely understand. Anyone have a bucket?

## CUin5

I was standing in my sister's kitchen when her phone rang. "Oh no!" She said to the person on the other end of the phone. Followed by, "Do you want to talk to your mother? She's right here." My sister, noticing that I was about to faint, had whispered, "Your son lost his cell phone."

Once I pulled myself off the floor, my mind began to race, wondering how long it would take to order him a replacement.

Within minutes, my son had gathered a posse to search for his missing cell phone. Interestingly enough I had just the day before gone over the cell phone bill and my eyebrows rose when I saw how many hundreds of text messages transpired over the course of a month. I know this has quickly become a preferred mode of communication. Who has time for actual conversations anymore? Besides, I've been told, "texting" is much quicker. It is? You should see me text from my cell phone. By the time I've scratched out a "C U in 5" I could've been there already.

Most of the time I get half-way through writing a text, and give up and yes, make that phone call from my cell even though my sons, nieces and nephews, even my sister have told me they don't really check their cell phone messages, but mostly use their phone to text. I tried to reply to a text I received the other day while driving down the freeway. My dad, who was with me at the time, said he didn't think texting while driving was such a good idea. I concurred and tossed my cell aside.

As for my son's lost cell phone, after searching and searching for 45 minutes, someone casually asked him if he'd looked in his car. "My car?" he repeated. Well, no, he hadn't looked there. Sure enough, there was the missing cell phone.

I asked my son if this was some homework assignment to see how many people he could get in a short amount of time to hunt for a lost item. He laughed and said I'd been "Punked." Then he quickly replied, "Just kidding, Mom."

I asked my son if I could write about this. "Sure," he said.

"I will," I said. "I will."

# Kitty Moments

He walked by me, stopped, turned around, and gave me the "evil eye."

Sitting in my mother's kitchen, I noted his improvement of behavior. "He didn't attack my leg this time."

"He likes you," my mother responded in a reassuring voice.

Now, I'm usually not afraid of cats, in fact, as a former cat owner (before she went to kitty heaven) my family and I were proud cat owners. But this particular longhaired black cat does instill some fear in me. When he wants to be fed, he'll attack your leg, and you better darn well feed him. Not only that, but if his favorite brand of cat food isn't laid out before him in his favorite bowl – look out!

Since our cat was laid to rest, it took some time to get over the loss. I couldn't walk down the pet food aisle without bursting into tears. At home, I couldn't walk by all her usual napping stations without imagining her there. I swore once after she passed away, I heard her meow.

We'd been through a lot with our cat. She was the third kitten we'd adopted in a week from the local humane society. The first one met an unfortunate demise when a wild animal attacked her and she ended up like, well…let's just say it wasn't for the faint of heart. Kitten number two was very quiet. Too quiet. She didn't run around like most kittens do. That should've been our first clue. When I took her to the vet, the vet took one look at her and asked, "How close are you to this cat?"

Enter kitten number three. At the animal shelter, she was doing leaps in the cage as if she were in the circus. Yup, she seemed to be a healthy kitty, and so she came home with us. For thirteen years, she brought us joy, even with her idiosyncratic nature; even when the vet diagnosed her with anxiety and she went to cat therapy and was prescribed medication. The Valium did help somewhat. (For the cat, not me!) She left us far too soon, and we all miss her.

We'll get another cat one day, or perhaps a dog. One thing is certain, there's nothing like having a pet to keep you on your paws…I mean toes.

# TTYL

I was too embarrassed to ask my niece from whom I'd just received an e-mail in which she signed off with <3 at the end, what that code meant. I'd seen the symbol before, and assumed it meant hugs or something like that, so I finally Googled it. The urban dictionary site where I was led to, explained that if you turn your head to a ninety-degree angle, you'd see a heart. HUH? Now, I have to turn my head sideways to read an e-mail?

Whatever happened to saying love you, love ya, or even, lu?

Kids! That's what's happened. They've created a new language. A language that I'm pretty sure isn't a class choice between taking either Spanish or French.

While software developers are writing their own codes, kids are busy creating and ever-changing their own symbolism. Probably so parents don't know what they're talking about!

When my father forwarded me an e-mail that he received from someone that had signed it TTYL, I wasn't sure what it meant, so off to Google I went.

Speaking of this urban language, LOL wasn't hard to get. That does mean Lots of Love. Right? And ROTFL means Ran Out To Find Lunch. Doesn't it?

Back to my dad for a second, he knew about Google before anyone had even heard of it. I remember him calling me, "You gotta use this new website, it's called, Google." My initial reaction was, "HUH?" Of course today, along with my daily dose of celebrity gossip, checking my horoscope and watching the news on-line, I wonder, how did I ever get through the day without the Internet, secret codes, Google and all?

I must run now, because I'm on deadline, and there's a rerun of Seinfeld on in the other room, one that always leaves me ROTFLOL, so I'll TTYL.

## Watering the Carpet

I was scanning news on the net as I do every day (ok, several times a day), and found this quote by Pope Benedict that said, it is important to, "…see the funny side of life."

Starting when my children were born, one of the many advices I was given from my mother-in-law was to find humor in raising her grandchildren. To find humor in raising children isn't always easy to do, case in point, when my then three year old unbeknownst to me, dragged in the garden hose to water the house plants, but was unable to turn off the hose and let the water run, and run, and run. Until my living room carpet was afloat in several inches of water. By the way, running water on carpet doesn't make a loud sound, a newborn however does, and as I was attending to the baby, the fact that my living room was turning into a lake, did skip my attention.

When I walked into the room and saw the carpet soaked, ironically my three year old was nowhere to be found. Could he have been the culprit? I called him into the house (I don't know for sure, but I think he was frantically trying to figure out how to turn the faucet off – in a hurry). When he looked at me with those innocent/guilty eyes, I took a deep breath, and his grandmother's wisdom came to mind, "…find the humor."

I knew at that moment, that moment when parents face a choice to yell and scream at their child, or yes, somehow find the humor, I chose the latter. Plus, as a bonus, the ruined carpet went and in came beautiful new hardwood floors.

So the next time you're faced with a situation dealing with your kids, or life, take a deep breath and as the Pope said, "…see the funny side of life."

# Disneyland Moments

"Don't you think a three-year-old is too young to take to Disneyland?" my aunt asked me over dessert and coffee.

I told her that when my son was three, I took him on his first trip to Disneyland.

"Yes, but did he get much out of it? -- Is it safe? -- Do you have to always be watching your kids or can they just run around?"

I was getting the feeling that she felt three was too young for a trip to the Magic Kingdom. She explained that her son, or was it her grandson, were going to take their kids to Disneyland, and I got the idea she didn't think that this was such a great idea, at least for the littlest Mouseketeer.

"How big is Disneyland? -- Are the lines long? -- Is it crowded?"

My aunt, who was visiting from Canada, pelted this California gal with questions before I could get the answers out from between bites of peach cobbler, which was delicious by the way (thanks mom).

I told my aunt that when my son was three we went in an entourage to Disneyland. The group consisted of my husband, my sister and her husband, and one precocious child.

We were flying somewhere over Los Angeles when my son peered out the window of the airplane, pointed at the lights of the metropolis, and gleefully shouted, "Disneyland! I see Disneyland!"

The next day when we did in fact arrive at the above mentioned destination, he ran, and I mean ran down Main Street, with me and the rest of the group in tow, running alongside him, as he pointed and shouted with delight until we reached the famed castle.

Yes, we had arrived at Disneyland. And now that we were there, he wasn't going to leave. He ran around that castle like there was no Tomorrowland. He ran through the corridors and back again. To him, Disneyland was the castle. The castle was Disneyland. And he didn't want to leave. So, we stayed, until he got hungry and decided a hamburger was in order.

Would I recommend taking a three-year-old to Disneyland? Absolutely. And the rides outside the castle ain't bad either.

# Soaring Kids

Children are amazing. You think you know them, but as they grow, they bring on their own unique personalities. What I've learned as I spent my years as a stay-at-home mom, is the joy of every day something that only a parent could understand - that children bring a sense of accomplishment, sometimes wanting to pull your hair out, but mostly the wonderment of watching them transform from helpless infants to the fly-by years of school age, and the (holding your breath) years of those infamous teenage years.

When they alas arrive at the college years, you may think your job as a parent is over. But in many ways it's just begun. The adjustment to college is a major life change. Our children need us less, but also in some ways, need us even more. Transitioning into adulthood can be a rocky road, but with guidance, and most of all the role models we have set as an adult ourselves helps them grow into strong, independent people, ready to face the world.

Families come in many shapes and sizes, whether at the helm, a single parent, a married couple, or any of the many other facets that make up the definition of family. Families that support their children through years of ballet practice, soccer, baseball, you name it, whatever their activities, will surely keep you busy raising children into becoming not the people we want them to be, but the people they want to become.

If as parents we've allowed our children the freedom to express themselves individually, we can pat ourselves on the back, because the time soon comes when they are ready to strike out into the world on their own terms, and they will soar like an eagle into the hemisphere of life.

## Cat People

We've been on the look out for a new pet for a while now, and keep vacillating between a cat or a dog.

I recently drove 260 hundred miles after a tip about an abandoned Cocker Spaniel who was in dire need of a good home. This would be our new pet! But alas, this pooch was to go elsewhere, and I drove home on an empty tank.

"What do you want a dog for anyway?" My sister asked. "You've always been a cat person."

I took umbrage at her remark!

We've owned our share of puppy dogs. There was Cocoa Chanel. But Cocoa loved to run into the street, and one day she ran straight into a car. Then there was Benji. Benji was a beautiful Golden Retriever. But he loved to dig holes, and eventually dug himself into more suitable living arrangements. Then there was Henry, a Sheltie, who loved to jump, fences mostly. He jumped right out of our lives and into someone else's.

If only we could find a dog that doesn't run, dig, or jump. As I reflect upon it, maybe my sister was right. Maybe we are cat people. But, we'll keep looking.

## Kids Tell All

Some day my kids will write a tell-all. Of this, I am sure. One chapter will detail how their mother's idea of cooking dinner is well, lacking. That their mother's idea of cooking is to: A. Burns it (This really is not done on purpose). B. To order pizza. C. Make pancakes.

Schools should not serve pizza. Why? Because pizza is an easy, quick and tasty choice for undomestic moms everywhere. Pizza remains our meal of choice. That is besides pancakes for dinner, which I tried to convince my kids was actually a dinner meal and not breakfast. But back to pizza for a minute. My kids actually gave me a cease and desist on ordering pizza. "Mom, we have pizza every day at school. Do we have to have it at home too?" Yes. Yes you do…

## Caller ID

The thing about Caller ID is - it works. The problem is, say for example you happen to be a night owl, or your baby has been awake all night with colic, and sleep finally arrives, at whatever hour, but wait -- then the phone rings. After you sleepily and with each passing second are increasingly annoyed, howl out, "You woke me!" And the person on the other end of the phone sheepishly responds, "I'm just returning your call." To which a ping-pong conversation ensues – who called whom first? "It says on the caller ID you called, I was just returning your call." To which you explain, "I was asleep, how could I call when I was asleep? Then your brain kicks in, "Did you check the date … the time of this alleged call?"

Of course, once the phone has awoken the baby, it's time to get up, no matter the time. And next time someone makes a phone call and hears a busy signal, well, perhaps it's just because the person did not hear the phone ring, or perhaps it's because the phone has been "inadvertently" taken off the hook.

# Tooth Fairy Moments

It was one of those hot summer days where I had found respite under a shade tree in the backyard. My two young toddlers were playing in the house ... but not for long. I heard a rumbling coming from inside. Soon, the noise became louder, finding its way outside and into my direction. There stood the elder of my sons with blood dripping down his chin.

"Look, Mom," he said proudly, as he held out his hand. There lay his first baby tooth. "I didn't know your tooth was ready to come out," I said. It seems it wasn't. He explained that his brother had "helped" it out with his foot. Thus, explained the rumbling.

I told my son about the tooth fairy, but he wasn't buying it. "There's no such thing as a tooth fairy," he said, adamantly. "Besides," he wondered, couldn't he "just get a toy?"

I begged him to believe in the tooth fairy, for my sake. My mind was racing. There has to be some make-believe left in the world. Have we televisionized our children to death with the harsh reality of life? What was next? No Easter Bunny? No Santa Claus?

I reiterated how if he left his tooth under his pillow, the tooth fairy would exchange it for money, and then he could buy a toy. After some negotiating, my son and I reached an agreement. He agreed to put his tooth under his pillow, and I got to believe in the tooth fairy … for a little while longer.

# The DMV

So it was that time when my Driver's License was up for renewal and unfortunately I had to take the dreaded written test. Fortunately my son, who at the time had just completed the driver's training course. We went to the DMV together, waited in line for two, maybe three hours (after two hours, who really counts?) All I know is I needed water bad and I'd already eaten my "emergency candy bar" in my purse.

We crawled our way to the front of the line. Being the wonderful mother I am, I let my son face the horn-rimmed glasses woman behind the counter first (okay, the she wasn't really wearing horn-rimmed glasses but perhaps if she hadn't been wearing glasses of some sort...) Well, never mind, I'll continue with the story.

With test in hand, my son traversed to the "Test Taking Area." This is a long counter where one shuffles the test around hoping the memorized answers will pop into one's head at any moment. I followed closely behind and perched myself at the counter space next to my son. As I glazed over the questions, I racked my brain to remember if a Class C license meant I could drive a 3-axle vehicle if the gross weight is less than 6,000 pounds? Or was it more than 6,000 pounds? I wanted to do a write-in answer ... you know, like when there's an election and you don't like any of the candidates running. My answer would be something like, "I don't even know what a 3-axle vehicle is, let alone drive one, so why are you asking me this?"

I was getting hot and sweaty when I decided that since my son, who seemed to be not sweating at all, had recently taken his driver's training, and he undoubtedly knew the answers, certainly better than I did. Especially since I hadn't read the DMV manual, I just breezed through it. That was my first mistake –not reading the manual. My second mistake came when I peered over and whispered to my son, "What's the answer to number 4?"

Two things happened next. One, I've never seen my son so annoyed with me (well, yes I have, but those stories would fill a book), and two, the bellowing I heard coming from the DMV clerk was not a friendly tone. "YOU THERE!" I looked around. Surely the roaring coming her way wasn't directed at me. Yup, it was. Suddenly I was wishing I had remembered to put my deodorant on, and the packed DMV, that seconds earlier had been a buzz with people chatting, now came to a complete silence as all eyes were on me and my reddened face. "YOU'RE NOT CHEATING ARE YOU?" The clerk was pointing her finger at me like it was a yardstick and she was a nun. "Ahh, no, I'm not," I replied, pretending I didn't know what she was talking about. "YOU MOVE AWAY HIM," she demanded, adding, "OR YOU'RE GOING TO GET THROWN OUT OF HERE." Now, let me tell you, I scooted away from my son, who by the way passed the test with flying colors. You see, he had actually read the book, and studied, and well, me, well I passed too, and not because I cheated but because I had to, I wanted out of that DMV fast.

# The Mommy Wars

I've heard rumblings around, and the sound isn't coming from an earthquake. It's the war of words between "alpha" moms and "working" moms. This new terminology of "alpha" mom frankly makes me want to puke. Every generation has a term for mothers, that chose or sincerely desire (and find a way to make it work financially – not just because they are rich and can afford to stay home) to be at home with their children. This generation is no different, but why oh why do we insist on pitting moms against moms?

In the not so distant past, "soccer moms" was a term that was bantered about by the media. As an aside, I don't recall a mother ever actually referring to herself by that term, it was some phrase made up because someone probably found the term, "housewife" or "stay at home mom" offensive. More recently the term, "baseball mom" is a term that I've heard used by the media. Now I have to admit that was a new phrase on me. Never heard of it, nor do I ever want to hear it again!

In fact, can't we all just get along? Why do we insist on branding mothers with labels at all? Moms are moms, wherever they work. And they should be just as respected for whatever choices they make in raising their family. And let's leave the cutesy and not so cutesy phrases in the dumpster and call moms what they are – moms.

# Letting Go

There's a thing in parenting…it's called "letting go."

While this concept may seem logical, it's also sometimes hard to practice.

From the time your little one starts kindergarten, it's a letting go process. It's not easy to watch them carry their little lunch box and off they go for the day to learn to spell, write, and tie their shoes. As a parent, you so desperately want to do everything for them. You want to tie their shoes; you want to push away that bully on the playground. You want to do their homework so they get straight A's and eventually get into that college of your choice.

Years go by and before you know it, you're attending their high school graduation. If your offspring goes on to college, those 4 or 5 years go by in a heartbeat. As they cross the stage to accept their college diploma, you're hoping your hard earned tuition dollars were not wasted. And most of all you hope your graduate will find a way into the world, support themselves and maybe even help to pay back those college loans.

Once your child turns 18, guess what? Even though you're paying the college bills, the airplane tickets back and forth for that long-awaited Thanksgiving or Winter Break; even though you've asked them about why they are taking Archery instead of Philosophy and have tried to find out if they are in fact attending class, what grades they are getting in college – guess what? You no longer have a say in their lives. You may like to think you do, but you don't.

When someone turns 18, they are now considered an adult. They can get married, they can vote, they are responsible for themselves and their actions, whether you like it or not.

So, when you're child turns 18, it's time not only for them to grow up, but also for you, as a parent, to grow up too. And remember, just because they are 18, doesn't mean they love and appreciate all you've done for them. Eventually (probably when they have their own kids) they will come around and thank you for everything you've done for them.

In the meantime, hang in their parents, and pour yourself a glass of something sweet, you've earned it.

## Jellyfish Moments

"It wasn't a big deal," my son said to me through the cell phone.

"It is a big deal."

My mothering instinct went into overdrive as he told me very matter-of-factly how he'd been surfing in the Atlantic when a jellyfish stung both his arms.

"Why didn't someone call me?"

As I was doing my own surfing through the Internet on jellyfish stings, I thought about when he fell off a 2nd story loft (or something of the sort), and broke his shoulder.

"It wasn't a big deal," my son had told me the next day.

"It is a big deal."

P.S. Thank you to the lifeguard who treated him for the jellyfish sting, and thank you to his friends who drove him to the hospital in the middle of the night when he broke his shoulder.

To a mom, these things, however minor, or seemingly major are big deals. We never quit being moms – ever. We are moms through and though. From the second our children are born to the second we leave the planet. And to mothers everywhere – that is a big deal.

## Advice from Son

There's a curious aspect about motherhood in which we enjoy giving motherly advice to our offspring. Yet, every now and then, our children are the ones who give us advice that's really quite remarkable. Actual words of philosophical insight that we ought to listen to and live by.

Some of these stated sentiments make one sit back and think about how quickly our children actually do grow up, and it makes me wonder... How did they get from diapers and climb up into the ivory philosophical towers in such a short, short time period?

It used to bug the heck out of me when people would say, as I struggled about with two babies still in diapers, "...children grow up so soon." I would think to myself, "...Sure, that's easy for them to say." Their children are already full-grown!

Then, just the other day, while talking to my son on the phone, he began waxing in a philosophical mood; his cell phone was on the fritz or something because I could only hear half of what he was actually saying.

But what I did hear, were words to live by. "Get out and enjoy life ... enjoy ourselves, whatever that is. You only live once, don't wait for tomorrow. When you wake up in morning, you can think it's going to be a really great day, or a really (expletive deleted) day."

So, following my son's advice, I'm going to say, "This is going to be a really great day." -- And I hope he gets a new cell phone soon, so I can hear more of what he has to say.

## Tattoo Moments

Okay, so I got a tattoo...I'm allowed, right? Wrong! I thought I'd surprise my family and hadn't told anyone, and so when a group of us were out to dinner, I wore a shirt that I knew would subtlety yet somewhat conspicuously show the newly acquired ink.

I couldn't help but wonder how long it would take anyone to notice the tattoo. Ten minutes? Five? An hour? Would anyone notice at all? Yup, before the waiter even brought the menus, my son glanced at me. And with a most horrified look on his face, he uttered, "Mom, is that a tattoo?"

Suddenly the chattering of family members and friends silenced. My other son, who was sitting at the far end of the long table, looked at me and his face said it all, but he repeated his brother's question almost verbatim adding a tone of disgust and disbelief, "Mom, you got a tattoo?"

I smiled proudly, "Yes. Do you like it?"

"What it is of?" An inquiring mind wanted to know.

My mind raced. I explained I had to leave to pick up Dad at the airport since his plane was coming in early.

"Wait!"

My sons weren't letting me go without further explanation and more precisely, they wanted to know, "What was I thinking?"

I insisted I had to leave, and so, slipping my credit card into my son's shirt pocket to pay for dinner, I made a quick get-a-away.

I arrived at the airport, picked up my husband and after arriving home; he tilted his head and asked, "Is that a tattoo?"

"Yes. Yes, it is," I said.

The following day, my husband bombarded me with questions. "Did it hurt? Where did I get it done at?" And most importantly, "What was the tattoo of anyway?"

Honestly, with this much fuss about my "tattoo," can you imagine what it would've been like if I'd actually gotten a real one?

## No TV, No Problem

I was a little stupefied when a friend of my son told me she grew up without television. I thoroughly thought she was kidding. She wasn't.

After counting aloud the number of TV sets we had in our house, I stopped at 5...okay 7, and wondered how one grows up without a television set. "We read a lot," she explained. "We listened to the radio," she elaborated.

As I thought about it, I guess it's not too hard to imagine not having television when most everything you want to read or watch is available with a few clicks of Internet.

I wonder if television sets will go by the wayside like the old-school monster computer monitors and the morning paper.

My father, not wanting to be outdone by someone growing up without a television set, piped in that he too grew up without one. "We only had a radio. From our farm in Saskatchewan, we'd listen to programs from around the world."

My father still listens to radio broadcasts from around the world, only now he listens to them via the Internet.

Perhaps the adage, the more things change, the more they stay the same has a ring of truth to it.

But I still like Seinfeld reruns, and you can't beat a good, I Love Lucy, you've seen a million times. And in the future, we'll all probably be watching them from the Internet.

Soon our TV sets will be obsolete, so maybe I should hang onto to one or two, just in case the Antiques Road Show comes to town.

# Motherhood Ironies

As I was leaving the grocery store today with my usual cartload of food, I glanced around for the bag boy (or girl) to help push the cart and unload the groceries into the car for me. Now, having just come from signing up for a membership at a gym, I pondered the irony of working out at an athletic club, yet wanting someone else to push the cart and unload the groceries for me. On the drive home, I began to think about this and other ironies in life:

- I'll drive around in circles at the mall until I find that perfect parking space, closet to the store, then go home and walk for two miles.
- Raisins? Yes, I like. Just not in any food.
- I'll buy a can of mixed nuts and pick out the pecans and savor each one.
- I'll let my hair grow so I can wear it long, but then pull it back into a ponytail.
- I love pickles out of the jar, but hold 'em in a hamburger or sandwich.
- I'll do laundry and then never put it away.

- My car has this funny way of detouring to the nearest In and Out Burger.
- To give my hair that "natural look," actually costs a lot of money.
- Chocolate cake is perfectly acceptable for breakfast, and pancakes are for dinner.
- Ask me for the phone number of my cleaning lady and I'll deny that I have one.
- I've never been to a professional football game, but never missed one of my son's high school games.

- I'll watch an entire Danielle Steel movie (for the millionth time) just for the last five minutes at the end when I cry my eyes out.

Sometimes ironies are just that – ironies. Sometimes though they make us laugh, give us convenience, and make us proud. Sometimes they cleanse the soul (like a good cry), and sometimes chocolate, anytime of day, is just what the doctor ordered.

## Highchair Moments

I admit it … I love being a mom. The great thing about it, is, I'll always be a mom, something I've tried to explain to my kids even when they think they are well beyond receiving any motherly advice.

I confess that I like being a mom so much that I can't wait to be a grandmother. Now, my kids are a long way from giving me grandchildren (Hey guys—anything you want to tell me?) But I do look forward to that day when I hold that little baby in my arms and I'll try not to impart words of wisdom until the baby is at least, well, let's say a couple days, no, a couple hours old…

I think my mother must've felt the same way because she had a highchair in our kitchen years before any of us (my siblings and I) had even thought about marriage, let alone having kids.

That highchair however, I think represented hope for my mom that some day there'd be a little guy or girl sitting in it. And, yes, years later there was.

I saw that highchair at my parent's house today. There aren't any babies right now in our family, but my mother still keeps that highchair in the house. The thought crossed my mind that perhaps I should grab that chair right then and there and sneak it to my house. I think the chair represents hope for the future, and we could all use a little hope, now and then.

# Please Enjoy the Music

The message on my cell phone was enthusiastic, "Mom, I see you finally figured out how to get music on your phone!"

You see, awhile back, I noticed when I phoned my son, instead of the usual ringing, I was directed by a pleasant voice, "Please enjoy the music while your party is reached." Then a song came on, one I recognized, a theme song from a popular TV show. I hung up and called him back. This time a hip hop song played, which I didn't recognize, but I really liked the beat. I called back a 3rd time, yet another song, a Journey tune, aah, a song from my generation. I liked all the songs I heard.

I asked my son if he could show me how to get songs to play on my cell phone. Yes, he said, he could show me how. It was easy. Would only take a few minutes.

Then I called my nephew about something, and I heard, "Please enjoy the music while your party is reached." I asked him if he could show me how to get songs to play on my cell phone. Sure, he said. It was easy. Would only take a few minutes.

Funny thing, neither one quite got around to showing me how to get songs to play on my cell phone. So, I spent several hours on the Internet, first of all trying learning the difference between ringtones and ringbacks, but alas, I finally figured it out. I have to say the hardest part was deciding which songs to choose. So now, when someone calls me, "Please enjoy the music…" And if you don't enjoy the music, either hang up, call again and get a different song, or better yet hang up and don't call back!

# Taking Care of Grandpa

The phone rang at 7:50 a.m. Of course I didn't hear it. However, I must've subconsciously because I woke up soon after at 8, an oddity for me that early, and as I staggered out to start the coffee brewing, I noticed the message light flashing on my phone.

Wondering who had called so early in the morning, I quickly checked the Caller-ID and saw the number was from my parent's house. My mother had left a frantic message at 7:50 a.m. that she "wasn't sure what it was, but something had happened" to my dad, and she was taking him to the emergency room. The blood drained from my body. I immediately phoned my sister to see if she had heard anything, and when she hadn't, I was careful in my choice of words. I didn't want to alarm her, and I told her I'd call her back as soon as I had any news.

I've never dressed so fast in my entire life. As I drove to the hospital, I kept telling myself to stay calm; that the reason my mother had taken my dad to the emergency room could be anything from, heaven forbid, something very serious, to a stubbed toe. I prayed for the latter, and took deep breaths and tried not to panic as the cars on a normally traffic-free road became like snails slithering down a garden path.

I hadn't realized how haphazardly I had parked my car in the hospital parking lot until hours later when I noticed that I had in fact taken up one and a half parking spots (sorry about that).

I ran into the hospital looking for the ER. Very scary thoughts ran through my mind. Was he dead? Had he had another stroke? Had he just tripped in the garden and needed a few stitches? But, there was a tone of fear in my mother's voice on the voice-mail, a tone that told me this was serious.

When I saw my mother, she was obviously relieved to see me and then announced that they would only allow one person in the room at a time, and since I was there, she would put me in charge. After all, she had weeds to pull at the Senior Center, a task she does as part of the local Rose Society. I guess we all react to things in a different manner, but I was thankful to learn my father's diagnosis thus far wasn't too serious. I mean if my mother took off with my dad waiting in the ER then I felt a cup of coffee was in order (for me).

When I returned with the coffee, I asked the nurse if my father could have some also. She said, "Absolutely not!" After all, he may be having surgery for an aneurysm. Somewhere between my mother leaving and me getting coffee, things had taken a scary turn for the possible worse.

A very long day ensued, which basically amounted to a comedy of errors; with my father telling people along the way, "My daughter's a writer. She'll probably write about this…"

At one point, an unnamed source whispered to us that she would like to tell us her experience in the ER. It seemed a particular doctor wasn't exactly as well liked and adored as the fictitious "Dr. McDreamy" on Grey's Anatomy. But then this was not TV. This was real life.

After a long day of tests, more tests, and even more tests, my father was discharged. My mother never did get those weeds pulled that day. And as I helped my dad into the car for the drive home, I smiled. I was ever so grateful with the knowledge that he would be able to read this column, as I would write about it just as he had proudly predicted.

# Flying Pennies

A fellow mom recently confided in me that someone had asked her... No, told her, "Not to talk about her kids so much." As she relayed this story to me, I was speechless, which is not an easy feat for this writer. I was baffled. This mother doesn't talk about her kids any more than any other mom I know. Her candid remark started me thinking. "Do we, as mothers, talk too much about our children?"

From the minute they're born, from the minute someone knows that they are going to have a baby, we as parents generally go ecstatic. I mean, Tom Cruise wasn't jumping on Oprah's couch for nothing.

And so it begins. Discussions with people offering advice, everything from what brand of diapers to use, right into deliberations on how to get your, up-and-coming, offspring into the "right" school. And I'm not just talking preschool here. Colleges are discussed with fervor and magnanimous expectations. Heaven forbid if your child doesn't get into the perceived-proper preschool, how will he or she ever get into an acceptable grammar school? And that is a direct lead into the appropriate high school, which will surely get them into the "right" university. And so we discuss. We banter. We debate. And, yes, we talk about our kids.

Talking about our children is a positive exchange of information. Indeed that's why we call our best friend when our children make us proud, or rattle our nerves.

I once strolled into the hallway and had to duck-and-cover because my sons were having a coin toss. No, not a coin toss like at a county fair where you merrily toss coins hoping to land on a plate in exchange for a stuffed animal or small trinket. No, I'm talking about pennies flying through the air like Major League baseball pitches. It's times like these, when a mother picks up the phone and calls her best friend, or her sister, or a fellow mom, or someone who will understand and listen.

So… Yes. Mothers do talk about their children's antics, the good, the bad, and even their penny wars. What a wonderful thing to be able to discuss the zaniness and blessings of motherhood. And believe me; I wouldn't change that for all the flying pennies in the world.

# About the Author

Catherine Burr is the co-author of the bestselling parenting humor book, *Motherhood is not for Wimps,* and is a prolific novelist. She is a multi-nominated Blogger's Choice Award recipient, has received an Outstanding Author Award and is in the Author's Hall of Fame. In addition, Catherine Burr is a noted North American Domestic Humorist. Catherine lives in California with her family where she enjoys every motherhood moment!

# Acknowledgements

I thank my children, Timothy Jr., and Daniel who propelled this writer to write even more! I was always a writer, but after the birth of my first child, I was compelled to capture every moment in writing. I love being a mom and when my second child was born, 18 months after my first, well, I didn't have as much time to write, but when my kids both started school, I took a sigh of relief and went home and cried because I couldn't believe my babies were growing up.

It's not easy being a mom but it's truly the best job in the world, and I wouldn't trade it for all the *New York Times* bestsellers in the world!

This book stemmed from columns I wrote for the Celebrity Café.com, which I won Blogger's Choice Award nominations in several categories. I want thank everyone who read my column and voted for me, you rock!

A wise person once told me to find the humor in raising kids, and I thank her that wisdom.

In *Motherhood Moments,* I share with you some of my favorite times as a mom. I hope you enjoy every moment!

Love, Catherine.

## Books by Catherine Burr

Motherhood Moments
An Inconvenient Attorney
An Inconvenient Mistress
Inconvenient Affairs
Jack and Jill
Desires and Deceptions
Orchids to Die For
Silicon Secrets
Wreal Writers Write Romance (contributing author)
Misadventures of Moms and Disasters of Dads (contributing author)
Motherhood is not for Wimps

www.ingramcontent.com/pod-product-compliance
Lightning Source LLC
Chambersburg PA
CBHW071624040426
42452CB00009B/1475